T0160681

FAR OUT WEST

FAR OUT WEST

CLARK COOLIDGE

ADVENTURES IN POETRY

The author thanks the editors of the following magazines
in which some of these poems first appeared:
Combo, Lungfull! and *Sal Mimeo.*

Cover photograph by Lee Friedlander
from *The Desert Seen*
Courtesy Fraenkel Gallery, San Francisco

Adventures In Poetry titles are distributed
through Zephyr Press by
Consortium Book Sales and Distribution
www.cbsd.com

& through

SPD: Small Press Distribution
www.spdbooks.org

9 8 7 6 5 4 3 2 FIRST PRINTING

ADVENTURES IN POETRY

NEW YORK 🐞 BOSTON

WWW.ADVENTURESINPOETRY.COM

ISBN 0-9706250-4-9

Contents

FAR OUT WEST

RIVER OF NO CONCERN

Nothing but blue sky and dinner bells
all the rest of your lumpy life
sometimes men take worms for steak
lovely to see you Lady Doubleyou
let's let our folks loose of these caves
make a farm out of the lead in your arms
did you like what you did?
lift up that ball don't let it dip
oil it and stagger away
take some stuff off
SALOON: TABLES FOR BADDIES
listen to those boreal choirs
these cat boys are like cattle to a toad
I'd better stop and pan some vitamins
see how gold comes off in the water
take off in a coffin and get away forever
or lurk in some of those famous forests
without a shirt

BAD HAND TERRITORY

Hello sheriff, give me another nose
or I'll give you one, one
guess that'll do it
what's the matter with that hole in your side?
if that wasn't true I wouldn't feel this way
goodbye
meanwhile the town is lit up like Poxie's Ledge
men, spread out into the resistances
there'll be no sweller vigilance
don't make me sway this town
resigned to beat a new retreat
all right boys this town's another place
let's stop grabbing the same man
I'll stop him with this banister (bassinet)
whoa! he just shot Gabby dead
well I think this town is going to stop
now were you really a member of the Dalton Gang?

BRAND WHAT

I was naked
then I came home to the House of Earrings
this was the Year of Those Bright Riggers
see the Collected Poems of Roy Rogers
Canyon of the Skull passages
lying down and going to sleep under a gong
filled with water
Storm Hand my only sultan
and Jimmy the Master of Silence
also Master of the Noble Acids
maybe wave away those mountains
if nobody puts a tail on my ass
don't make me wet as dirt
here is the closing mind
both barrels when the saw teeth come together
the old west must be speeded up
at least by a cow length
or soon we'll come to
the Rock That Stands Like a Beast in a Tree
where the enemies are little boys
but they last as long as the stones

FAR OUT WEST

Among the blades were deer statues
froggies and their things
blue acts as placement tends to arrive
the elevated hearties don't care
they come in bars and prude wastes
bladder dreamers on cushions they mar
now I don't have to laugh at
these tiny planets then suddenly I do
aren't we all relatives of the big blackboard?
nothing so tantalizing as a billy goat's squares
stop drawing with your cigarette
but nothing quite overhangs the piano
like billy's bag
give me a quart of those puzzle weights
the people are all fuzzy
are there any peppermints left on earth?
not a picture but a framed nothing
and a red light at the end of your cue
these people I think were stored
like that hero out of teak wood
not as if the words for anything were hard
here we'll pretend to find muzzlelips
I came across Clinton at a wayside lunch
is this the country where everybody's gone home?

Clearingville pop touché
where there's mutton
a bell on the formica
and nothing but a head at the window
these memories of a golden
but we've passed all the greener streets
and friends with lights on
they live above all these neon plugs
but what did you expect?
the whole town's bed wetters

Right About the Running Woman

Vienna's tits are made of
slats from wood casks
and the colored stratigraphy is a set
people don't believe in anything
when they're lit
when they shrink
and there are thin rods in the way
the street is for dogs
and for amplified visible harmers
so be it
close tongues at the skyblue bank
and the clay hero is always "Johnny"
put your dough behind green doors
and claim savvy
too much dust in the pursuit of knobblyness
and red pumpkins written on by orange pens
are you fragile?   basta
habit the enemy of story
nothing left in these chromium mines
but steps up to the mike and skips
and slips and slaps himself
the passle rides out under cambric skies
I'll be first
a basket sandstone of all inverted echoes
and rootlessness in dusty blasts

this is itchy men with big
fingers and toilets on their saddlehorns
these woods are going to be full in a minute
they say I opened up on myself
on the rise by every stream
brace yourselves
there's nothing like prime American ugliness

DOWN TOO MANY BARRELS

Those boys on the roof are just
waiting to fall through
but that bartender's kind of awkward
chairs full of young whiners and sod galoots
some other Jasper says I'm dull
eye like ball of scum
was that a liquid on the plate?
one churl set sail for New Bedford
but I've kept my Butane attitude
Butane Nevada that is
bottle full of oiled monkeys this is
there's an old saying: when the wine is done
you just have to finish it
makes sense to me a flush bunny
even down dark alleys of mirth
get your hooks off them potatoes
the town suffers from roundup
here come the miners minus dollars
want to be diners bright
as a dime on a cancelled stamp
but all these bellies are empty
as a star on a tom fool
and I'm sick of this dirtbank living
think I'll get me a sack
full up with bendable goods
one hand faster than a twisted dog

the other from cyclone load
but this sheriff's getting his sides mixed up
hey this card table smells like the sea
better ask Bill Hackleroad
he's in charge of the chloroform board
the jail's filling up with lead weights
Notion Boys hard as empty boxes
reach and go blind in this town
Robert Ryan can't see beneath
the cowboy stairs and what bodes
won't be long now

THE PRICE OF SCABIES

At Dragoman Bay Pike claims
your brightness is showing
the rest all clamping down
argh   bad samples
but these guns will come out
snapped Glass making his play
hold your vent coat?
take no time to blink
Apostles they call these pasty cardmen
meanwhile the deputy whittles
little copies of the coffee service
he talks like undersea
Whit Bissell hawks buggy paint
wheels and chews out the whole town
folks cut down like a missing load
but Curly got caught upstairs
a suicide in a butt of milk
I need a place tight as a copper stamp
watching folks' skin roll off like futures
sure as a pencil-white hole
seems only the law wants to know
has the call come down
for a brand new slate?

ALL DRESSED OUT IN STORM
(A CHARNEL WHIP)

Sterling Hayden's working on a lacy delirium
a bluntness the long and shirred of which quells
firms a plastered lacquer shell on tap
I would have died if you hadn't come back
in these gaps have done with the Damn Quick Kid
I heard enough Barreltits shut it close
a diamond diameter with a look from Vienna
the clasp of a human jacket then harmless kisses
so half-lit the Stooges bend over don't flinch
this cuttletown is drenched in coffee and cards
dog dirt and remembrance gules
a green glass door so thin the small rocks beyond it
the large man with his candlepower guitar so hangdog
a shirt sleeve left?   open the door so dumb
comes hope to the Calcium Travelers
Old West vanished New York smelled of fish
an egg for Ernest Borgnine his beater shredded too
the very walls of leather won't stop a slug
strapping humans on the rock-dealt porch
but this valley is no home
who'll blow holes in these stolen teams?
a silver mine that can't stand
the mollusk at its rim

PEGLEG HOLDEM'S DEATH

I've gotta get that rimrock furnace turned on
yes and Steve of the Canyon to help out
bonds of steel are forged in these sandy draws
classics like storm helmets lined in dryness
I'll just hold onto these molecules while you roll
what are they doing with those riders?
probably buckle if you leave 'em and
shake another trap quick by getting out
your black vest and herd pass to show 'em
sound by Earl Sitar
now they all gather to watch Windy pinch his eyes
afraid the whole town's gone stout
saloon's just another waste of glass
not too many weeks left in the county entire
guess it's time to bring Blackie back from the wheel
but like Cassidy says You never can tell
this dust-ball town might suffer from
the red big toes of Morrie Ankrum!

YOU DON'T TELL ME

This one is about guys leaning on buckboards
try making trouble with your own brother
this railroad won't hold guitars
see that missing chunk of DeNiro
the boss keeps pictures of himself in his pants
Hoppy can't believe in the droopyness of human ken
depending on any boulder he's smaller than
the shadow of a penciled-in cayuse
he's horrified at the mere idea of a boneyard
the only tale with a fossil doctor badguy
but you can't wear glasses in rock territory
and catch a whiff of the Cattleman's Association
keep your eyes peeled on those buttes
don't let the herd break that way
here comes that passle of lurking dynamite
hard as a tree and I reckon it's got popular
or a windy liaison in ranting clusters
now get Sidearm on his feet now pick his flaps
the lard eyes of realization overcome him
there's an obvious sky here by cracky!
let the lungs out of your horse
the gloom from your weapon
hard to tell fresh donuts from protective slabs
all arbitrary figures beneath
the Mountain of the Holy Cross
or a twice-as-windy draw, one

PROFESSOR HEPBURN RIDES AGAIN

Sitting in poison BVDs near a pot of rocks
at Satan's Ballyard
I heard my play and made it
no loaded boxes to cram these clefts
who knew an old goat could trot like the wind?
but a mighty fluid holster'll do ya
just keep your hands away from that brain
a rag full of Guinness and you're tan as a soak
hey, run away from those sticky rocks!
can I borrow that skull with the slug in it?
a henchman named B. Lacky walks so slow
aims to fit like a stone in a tombstone
this outfit's credited with plenty of lurks
beeves all shown in a line at Hoofplant Station
this'll ring a trim load next
property of MacLane Buttee
known to farm out his weapons
favor any old pile of stones
in vistas of wraparound dynamite
now just hold on and I'll shoot somebody

A Plain Load of Dumb Luck

The boss's name is Ranchline
mainly he pulls pickles in barrels
there are charges
stepped to the window and blotto
next there'll be poesis on a gameboard
what makes you think then
the world will start to gel?
obvious stocks of serial things abide
but not so's you'd know it eh?
carried Clay out and took a bromo
with the will to stop storing things
I thought you saw it through
the one that landed
then put the director home in bed
who walked the perimeter in visible leggings
no one can stop thinking like these are
the weathered frames of Royal Dano

FOR A DECENT MAN YOU SURE GET A HARDON SHERIFF

Let's hit the road
no further sheets to be lit
apply the Lysol
test the mettle of wood
the white hat out of wood
the nervous sign and the mineral drops
Benny? get me the Foam Vampire
business fragments that come in a box
another breath and the rafters are full
but these people hang together in rooms of speech
take that Yeats song and ride it
the last time you're in bed
the goods of a lifetime come due
look in your room it's frightening
like the basements of the Golden Empire
disc of a world that glows and spins
a bare field with its leading vocalists

THE BATTLE FOR THE COTTON RESERVES

Trucked his way through a door and grasped glass
the colonel is a maniac
I'm a store-bought flake
jackass runs me in blue
Indians hate illuminated buttons
lace-drawn windows oubliettes
get off my plush
domestic life even on the frontier is
boring and repetitive
the copse is laden with sand duration
I drunk   I lie
wash my teeth with radioactive clams
actor, our lives can't be bought this cheap
and now nothing is left but the fire fossils
that's a good shine when do I leave?
Paladin commences   the Dude abides
including President Dent
I lived in the house with the back
of the battle miniaturized
there are ores there
scoop the love from your innards
late of the Big Sioux Lull

HANDS UP SO FAR

Get that glass off my bed
without bowing
then go on a bender
nobody's telling you what to do
but be careful this town's
spine's broke like a water main
big men end up in small cemeteries
but I'd hate to humble myself
to that size of hair
and I won't kill where I can't smell
where these big deal gunfights
are tiny breakthroughs
now that tightwad kid's gone plug
a matter of war and odor
let's have ploughboy drinks at the Partial Bar
watch these boys play bones with dry hats
take rumpled falls down stairs
as bad aim tends to settle things just as well
the Flannel Boys make their plays around beds
get thrown and don't even lose their cigarettes
once upon a time when nobody's business is coffee
while the shirts wait in rooms with tingling rods
and the court comes to a big human state
of golden standards and empty beehives

THE GRIMACE AT STONE JUNCTION

It's so bright in the old west
the people look smaller in their livingrooms
things to happen "any hour now"
but it's all laundry bright
so the whiskeys look like colas
nothing but dry hats till you drop
and the guy I just shot's still looking at me
over the damp rump of a chestnut
as skin babes in Chinese brocade slide behind walls
guess brick skulls don't come cheap
so put up red planks and suppose nobody can reach you
I'm a Johnson but I think like a pin
the town's basic lawbooks are full of hot water
I'll come around later when I'm better
but this west is too close-up
too much glass itching to smash
I'll have to go down and call out Joe Rile
this dust crate Summer of the Badges
I know sullen teens can't hold down grey jails
let the bellrope lamps hang blood-red
nights when the blind draws subside
but this'll all look better over
my allotted morning portion
puddled then handled like a slab

Outlaw with Sand

Has Scapa Flow slid to Deep Dish America?
nodules or pussy which is it?
gents have never exited these halls
creases in the face near merchandise in place
Blood Butte is where
I weep at my lack of control
fuck you there's nothing under an empty skull moon
but for now the Earth is a going place
and I own the fall leaf concession
it's fine but here the Cross is the name of a bar
nowhere in this universe is there any forgetting
but it's all forgettable as any clam
dry your eyes   exit the pod
divorced from the one with expectations
I have no overcoat
and stranded all my crystal thoughts
a book is the sore result
in a territory without radio
the outlaw is a sustaining man
some hand on cold steel pisses off

THE RASH COMPONENTS OF SKIP HOMEIER

Too many rock chips in these Merican flaps
no more of this fast fist and hard gun
the skin had come off close to those buttes
these bad ones walk right out and right back in
cute as that   a driller with few doubts
got to have a hot-head making his place before I will
Gun is my name steel shanks and belts my game
we live in a brusk country you should know better
get that axe and be careful I'll break with knowledge
daylight all the time here the horses tip sideways
because there's no sidewalks we pretend it's a town
but the hero insists he's seen atoms
a bubble where his neckerchief should be
now no one will dare ride him
this looks like a job for somebody who's in another movie
Hoppy?   a gang call themselves the Land Cancelers
watch out for their way with the west
Hardscrabble Caverns their hideout at this rate
nobody's name will be left
but suits the one who quits

THE PUISSANCE OF STRING TIES

Go up some stairs
outside of the building always
turn right turn out all right
the whining of boulders past my kitchen
you'd need the embrace of butters
glass coming down patter
of daylight on the skull
maybe fill that hotel full of lead
and a bullet crushes the watercooler
(in a western?) has to stand for something
why these sliders are bucket wimps
now take off your complete outfit
this is like being trapped in a standing lamp
nothing but soda crackers on paraffin stoves
somebody said so in these buildings
but now the town's all sewed up
this from some pitiful runouts
sky blending like paint over the next ridge
these are the Blundering Gunslingers
too late for supper
too close for brains
and this is the Iodine Kid

RIDERS OF THE BOARDS

The populace disgruntled in chairs
outdoors there's suspicions
on the trail comes Harpo in a bandage
we have to see about it climb
stairs in the days when paint
give me your clothes put on a sack
a town shot by back-a-ways drillers
the hero is always the shortest hand
but isn't it too sunny for bullet death?
they say the ore was too light for gunplay
but these boys just waded into each other
the gang put the Chinese cook on top of Harpo!
and the town came down with wooden stains
no parlor in the whole lot but cattle space
autumn already and nobody hospitalized
remember Trouble at the Line Shack?
this time the violator is named Strange
so the boys start coming down like stones
the numbers off a set-to and a big one
one rife with contusions Harpo's inventions
have to ride out of town with your brains
between your legs stack up
your own bloody case of erosion
as the hero crosses a whole street of intentions

EARNEST TAMPERS

A heart full of mortar and a skin full of dynamite
there's a dildo on the horizon
Hoppy's suspicions are prevalent
the bad ones here use "optical" dynamite
I'll kill every fool in this room
those steely eyes can't be flirted with
but he's a man (doom)
I'll agree to whatever you say (darkness)
laid at the base of a buffalo cypress
why he just smashed up a case of meat
do they do crosswords on the prairie?
naw but sometimes
the voice of a boar insists
so we fall home after the evening rustling
and the hacienda's mine but it's
Hoppy's horizon three coats of cement
at every point (Hoppy's disappointment)

Trustworthy Locator with Dog

It seems Hoppy raided the tile factory
they had a good supply of oats there once
consult the math-green Rollodex of plan

Hoppy took a weekend to hike up his pants
broken silhouette of cog meat in the wind
see tumult

Then Hoppy ganged up on the other feeders
shards of the leash rule lay strewn
it's in the bucket

A lame imitation of Hoppy by Windy
throne room broken into flame gone
you'd have to toss your digs

And lastly Hoppy has vacated the moon
his new fall line of Fisticuffs to Fussbudgets
you all come down

TOWN GONE OFF
(ROCKS MADE OUT OF RAISINS)

That town burned down
just close your eyes
checkerboards line the saloon so
the cigar man wouldn't or won't
a questionmark cloud over this slot
but the boys're all lathered up
now watch for that cross-up bunch
they *stroke* their cattle
when everybody's back is turned
might have to shoot myself some milk
now put that house out
see his mustache blow off?
caves below these hills in a silver rain
drove his horsie right to the granite
that one keeps on mixing in
for part of this one Hoppy's a brown-noser
too many sleeves in these rocks (beep)
now a ten-penny silence in the Land of Trees
they got Fisher!   I'll get him!
no big thing leaving odd men dead on the land
a lot of clay in these Big Windies
white as tea in a stonebreak
but they'd have to pretend Hoppy's no good
you say this Hoppy's marginal?
about as romantic as the empty dust

The Drawbacks of a Riderless Valley

See Hoppy dance at the Wingchair Room
woody-headed as a dying duck in a thunderstorm
hope he don't die out nice
now how'd they get Rauschenberg to play Lucky?
what they need is the Brylcreem Joiner
in amongst the Puddle Officers
but the kid's in trouble again (runt)
go get your head and I'll settle the horses
now No-Jacket Cassidy hangs his gun on a rose tree
and the boys all mosey over to see it
laugh of a questionmark cow
Lucky can't tell a valley from a desert
but these boys just love saying things
a sound of dry-gulchers working themselves loose
as that skunk moves up Hydrophobia Mountain
and the ranch girls go green
there's too many rocks under this sun too many windows
glares in the lake and says Let's stop and think
these road agents 'bout to die of their own reservations
the rest got the license to boil
notice how the weeds don't move

THE BIG SUNDRY

These rocks are the salt of the soul
mortice of the faceted dude
have you seen Open Lemon Stomach Canyon?
tendrils of guns rule here
dry bones of a mortician's picture
now brace your tits here it comes
or is this White Liquor Canyon?
a parade of epsom salts leads these pipsqueaks
hardly a savory bunch too many grains
in the bloodstreams of all pesterers
dumps blow up in this plain old west
fish heap or no devil spoon
watch this tiny Heston Peck machine crank
till the stars come home
property reduced
skulls grown ripe
thoughts come dense but no denser
than a bruised knee in Crayon Canyon City

CATTLE ON HORSEBACK
(A METHODICAL THINNESS)

A brightening Hoppy stops just in time
reins in before the crime
Coronas, boys? he hands back their iron
thought I propped you all back up in our lamer days
just another desert hill in a row
grins at the thought of dressing somebody down
on a range gone sour you better mind your trips
balances apples on a sittable saddle
spends that whiskey like shadows on a wall
give me a lift into the bedroom, boys
got to dry out his white horse on an autumn ranch
just out of autumn's reach (flinch)
but these are pretty tall fools what do we do?
nice piece of granite put it in your pants for later
there'll be no more run-outs on this side of town
or bronze keys for the blue ledges
a man could go far in that shirt
seems this gang got stuck at Lovable Buttermass
a dream time home with no hard songs
guess we'll have to stay strangers
and well, stinginess is okay but his boots stick out
and there's been too much blending of trails
I tripped!
now Cassidy enters darkly
hears a bottle rattle on a table
just the place for a jump-off
and gets to go off

Higher Saddles and Shorter Ladders

He just brought a horse out of that building
can't be long now till fire hour
rockhewn pig over by closed old stove
seen anyone waving in this weary country?
hey I think I hear the light coming
commits a boner at the line shack (mopery)
get me something to eat   that's tellin' 'im boss
then the gang thought twice spineless and counting
wheel stains on the angle door and then some
here comes that wandering varmint with the hole in his sack
best go back east where they all wear wide pants
now they all stay low to watch that candle tighten up
it's a cinch that nobody's taken care of
like a huge cavern in the mind
a horseload of rock as bonus
whole town turns out to see the bungstarter arrive
shoot him and make him say "oh"
only losing time pointing pencils
guess your icehouse days are over
signed one Alan Bridge as Norton (badguy)

ONLY POSSIBILITIES

The shadows blur across Oxening Yard
but these are staples and so seasonal
remove words until you stroke bare walls
people wear vests and say it's the west
like lines in the face occupational dropsy
you'll have to rip hairs from your forehead
it's the law of bacteria to stay until
the connections are metal on cloth
whole tales about "the sense of it" drear
subtitle the Dalton Gang Meets the Chairs
but I'll have whatever you're talking about
some need whiskey some glass evidently
there was no voice over
that old west

Occasion Killer

A rocket entered the old west
was velvet spacial lumpish nod
somebody will speak instead of dying
a blizzard of rocks sets coma
the gnawing of blood from sand
but the desert was far from stellar
a so-so space I guess says
Stimy Boteach the Illini letch
the walls all a ponder of fungus
the funereal hills sidereal
but the west was more leveled than most places
gossipers lived on multiple stages
grotesqueries where clocks were candies
and a slug on a rock your only margin
I was supposed to witness the comet
from Summit Ridge Deck but
these codgers went shopping for pictures
of an agate contained an albumen specimen
in the Drome of the Clustered Stems
I'll drink to that node
my buddy was the Molybdenum Kid
an optical here that does no good
a telling of the nothing left

FROM THE CIMARRON SANDHILLS

They don't like the smell of rope
need a new uniform?
watch that onion form
got strung up on a mineral farm
flash of sun on a lowcut neck
man named Sam dubbed Territory Badman
hear that music in the sand?
now it's all cord suits and bank ties
a sodality fit for Abernathys
this town on wheels rolled over the hill
the one with the tassels
and bells and nothing could be called law
guess I'll ride over in my blower suit
with ten tabs of Billerica Blue
just home down east where
even the whistling stops

I Said the Duck

Bullets in a gun remind me of tub thumpers
mind you the grey leaks fast from reward
otherwise amazed at the indoor stars
crops that stall the equipage of animals
I clip all my items from the Quarry News
where that kid kept his livery from lottery
otherwise it's tear-ass all the way to the future
and hobgoblin beyond just taste my word
the sealant it is to be needed given
a host of scarlet horizons three pots and a post
peel the skin of nightriders slung out a ways
the wooden cover over promptness that lingers
that it's one man's bag as tells the tale
slow on the way to the chair wall or none
a notion to? not experienced enough
and off a league or so from solid
the light from that stone won't do you
but bullet dreams leave a kind of sand
you'll think you'll need sans stars
or a roof over your brute beliefs
sprung from a race of shovelers
stubborn as the standing tomb

for David Peoples

DOUBLETALK ON TUMBLER'S FLATS

Here comes Ma Wood and her nesters
with murder in their eyes
Barbwire Knobby playing 'round with fence posts
kinda noble on the mind but mixed in water
ends up in Andy's apple pie

The small scale rocks turn out to be huge
rim rocks the riders call 'em
down below Barrel Wells the nesters form
card wranglers to the sky old army shells

Then Hoppy reinvents the natural day
unties his sidekicks too
it strikes him that death hides
somewhere up in those ledges
following the rules of lookout and lineshack

The boys get feeling kind of starvy
taking on faith in a shadowy entrance
heard there was fire in the cattle canyon
no standing on convention go bottle 'em

Guess this is the riding past
sort of funny rocks and drovers both
but Ma Wood's no goat
and Hoppy's all out of sticks

{45}

A MOON OBSCURED BY CLOWNS

Dietrich had a hobby horse
spotted
sung by Bill Lee
close-up by Dad Lang
this is Blow Country
hometown of the Sayer
a fly from the surface
the darks and lights of it
the Gundysons know
try Lulu at the Spigot
gunbearer on a lowered couch
is everybody down?   hanging
as quiet as eating a banana
few left that ride the Scouring Trail
a doorway stander made of stolen brass
and let the gate rot for all I
just let me out of these cardboard interiors
think time's stronger than a rope?
CHUNK!   that piano sounds like a potato tree
not to mention horses right indoors
and a species of moth too close to all this
empty revolver empty chamber
I'm just waiting for the diers to surface

STEALERS WAY WIDE

These boys can't wait to ride out and hand somebody
the revival of a stubfoot mental architecture
and the race is on for the rights to Pouchy Bend
look like nothing so much as horseriders to most
if you do that you're guilty of eternity
do what?　light out for the stony heights?
a place claimed by these dumb grazers
but owned by Shiny Eagle MacTeague
end of an era I 'spose the blunt end
dead or alive propped up below the Book Cliffs
and tough to beat as the stain on a snake
think you could reach?　I'll double back and watch
the territory turn turtle out by Horrible Walls
that's where we'll deal with the velocity of husbands
they'll bring on damage like an old boot
so the boys must hold out as I said
nowhere to go but sheer down
Quantrill from Tent City shot
and speeded up so signing off

GUN PLAY ON AN EMPTY STAGE

Hoppy's missteps are recorded in a glancing tomb
no wooden steps lead to this
Gang of the Chipped Dicks
that go off like hot leaves in the Annals of Dread
put a part in your head
a little property titled Hoppy Snarls
you think the sun's gone off at will?
this hotel's got nothing but rooms to back out of
so Hoppy stays put
his horse too white to stay clean
now watch the action come to a point
I thought I'd see something if only I'd
fossil of trouble here on the rise
you can see by this face the joints are closed
kick that buggy up   think
California will make it to California?
just sit tight and keep your story shut
a matter of hats on in the household
the boys want to learn how Hoppy balances
meanwhile a caterwaul has added to the to-do
breakfast?   in a nutshell
you can tell that bozo by the B.O. tattooed on his arm
well we'll be going
the point is tomorrow
to land on both feet
I got a petunia feeling
it's less painful to fire in unison

JAWBONE SHOVELS

These boys ride around timing tiny landscapes
for the paintings they'll do later
in a long line of mint pumps with close brushes
stop grunting like a pig the handle claims
nothing on these tables that can't be colored
with spiders could bite right through the glass
think this is just a front for coppers?
better butter up your end before it pales
dreams of becoming Master of the Canyons
well, all right   I'll just pull that tag
off the burial wall the plot's a weakling
a matter of baloney in smoke out at the crags
you could keep an eye on   oh, that
it's what's under your hat that I don't like
now you just get cozy while I unload this snake
much better to prize your own image
abuse yourselves while you can   I'm not
the formations he assembled will not go away
paste under glass buttes with peculiarities
and at the head of it all?
one with no further rocks to spy
the army thinks all rocks look alike
just a cribbage can full of stalemates

THIS YARN NEEDS A SLIPPERY FINISH
(NOISE OF THE PICKOFF BOYS)

I don't like to see human beings run down
a shack up in the rocks'll do the trick
but it's only Paper Jack is yellow
the gang takes on so much sunshine
they'll run over the water slick as a toe
I got the faucet rights right here in my pocket
set up by a pool called Cacker's Joys
guess the boys'll be loading up on Darvon
but there's always some Cassidy in Dutch
a responsible man's death in a trench
dark as a punching reckon
drape that ranch around your neck you pinch!
just noticed somebody's gun's exposed
rimrock victim of one wicked placement
well I figure he's young enough to get clipped
just a borrowed saloon in the weeds
towered over till the skin shows
and this rusty outfit rests on its beans
meanwhile Red's practicing his Chinese beckon
I think the strawboss needs a sawbones
wouldn't take much to make this whole valley wait
but now there are more rocks
than all the gathered weathers
Cassidy enters

Hombre Your Installments Are Showing

Hoppy wants to number all his bullets
like all the horses and cattle he's already numbered
and don't you just know it
the Indians are coming but Lucky's boulder rolls
down like that there's just no telling
Dragoons of Nodule Gulch as a setup
now let me borrow Victor Mature's ladder so I can mount
down the trading post boys it's run by flies
once Lucky's done pushing the Indians around
we'll have some mild romance
more than a few of these are surrepticious travelers
and still Hoppy hasn't showed since the count
but just look at how young his hair is
dusty as all these bosoms go
whatever you do don't show your hand
catch that Indian on trumpet this here
over behind that rock is a "drop"
no doubt the older west was slowest
guess that's the price of dewlaps incorrigibles
Hank D'Amico there shows some irons in the fire
think I'll go down and consult with old Eagle Cut
let Hoppy have his numbers this outfit
's about as funny as a fire brigade
you just watch out for those flashing hills

LAND OF THE PASSING STRANGE

Hoppy dumps his paregoric down the loo
makes as if to speak you know
you ought to shoot those things
they're dangerous as rimrock blackouts
drummers with thinner bags thundering
redeye gluggers the prices pasted on slabs
one with love and the other with food
now these bends will make us equal
meanwhile I'll duck out and find some tools
set off like baling wire in the wind
but the boys are fresh out of throats
aw that's just an old log table
testy mess of talk no matter the settler
says Gus is my name Mistrust is my game
just wait till the last leg of this journey
and the mine's been branded now so
drift on out till everything's hot and quiet
then saddle up boys 'cause Hoppy needs the altitude
needs it like his shadow on the wall
waving like a needle in the stone

Text set in Bodoni Book.
Book design by *typeslowly*.
Printed in a first edition
of eight hundred copies
by *McNaughton & Gunn*.